LIVING WITH
CYSTIC FIBROSIS

by Susan H. Gray

T H E   C H I L D ' S   W O R L D ®
C H A N H A S S E N ,   M I N N E S O T A

The Child's World®

The publisher wishes to sincerely thank Annie McKenna, M.S., R.D., C.N.S.D., for her help in preparing this book for publication.

Published in the United States of America by The Child's World®
P.O. Box 326
Chanhassen, MN 55317-0326
800-599-READ
www.childsworld.com

Photo Credits: Cover: Picturequest/Corbis, Custom Medical Stock Photo, Inc. (inset); Columbia University/Archives and Special Collections: 19; Lester V. Bergman/Corbis: 6, 14; Picturequest/Corbis: 1; David H. Wells/Corbis: 12; Custom Medical Stock Photo: 7, 8, 21, 22, 24, 26; Stone/GettyImages: 9, 10, 13, 18; Courtesy of the Kimberly Meyers Family: 16, 17; Cassy Cohen/PhotoEdit: 4; Mary Kate Denny/ PhotoEdit: 15, 29; David Young-Wolff/PhotoEdit: 23; Tony Freeman/PhotoEdit: 25

The Child's World®: Mary Berendes, Publishing Director

Editorial Directions, Inc.: E. Russell Primm, Editor; Alice Flanagan, Photo Researcher; Linda S. Koutris, Photo Selector; The Design Lab, Designer and Page Production; Red Line Editorial, Fact Researcher; Irene Keller, Copy Editor; Tim Griffin/IndexServ, Indexer; Donna Frassetto, Proofreader

Library of Congress Cataloging-in-Publication Data
Gray, Susan H.
 Living with cystic fibrosis / by Susan H. Gray.
 v. cm. — (Living Well series)
Includes index.
Contents: Shannon's story—What is cystic fibrosis?—What causes CF?—What's it like to live with CF?—How do we know about CF?—How do we help people with CF today?
 ISBN 1-56766-105-X
 1. Cystic fibrosis—Juvenile literature. 2. Cystic fibrosis in children—Juvenile literature. [1.Cystic fibrosis. 2. Diseases.] I. Title. II. Series.
 RC858.C95 G73 2002
 618.9'237—dc21   2002002867

TABLE OF CONTENTS

CHAPTER ONE

DO YOU KNOW SOMEONE WHO HAS CYSTIC FIBROSIS?

Shannon was a wiggly, playful baby. She loved her stuffed tiger.

She squealed when her big brother tickled her feet. By the time she

These young girls, like Shannon, love to have slumber parties.

was two years old, however, Shannon was coughing a lot. She had trouble gaining weight. When her mother kissed her neck, she tasted a little salty. Shannon's mom took her to the doctor.

The doctor checked everything and said that Shannon had cystic fibrosis (SIS-tik fy-BROH-sis). He told Shannon's mom what to do for the coughing and how to help her child gain weight. Now Shannon is ten. She likes to ice-skate and she loves slumber parties. She wants to fly airplanes when she grows up.

Shannon is one of 30,000 people in the United States with cystic fibrosis—about 1 person in every 9,500. Cystic fibrosis is often called CF for short.

CHAPTER TWO

WHAT IS
CYSTIC FIBROSIS?

Cystic fibrosis is a disease of the mucus (MYOO-kuss) glands.

Mucus is a fluid inside the body that keeps the organs wet. The

mucus glands are tiny pockets of **cells** that make the mucus.

Some mucus glands are inside your stomach and **intestines.**

That mucus keeps food moist as it passes through your body. Mucus

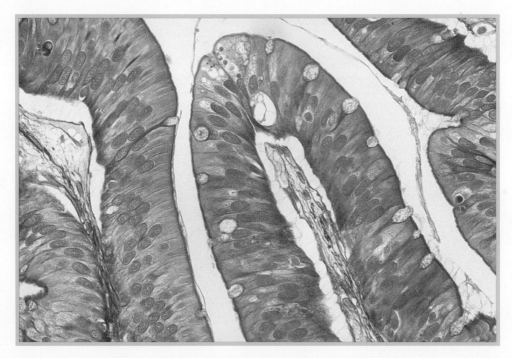

This microscopic view shows the cells that make mucus.

glands are inside your lungs, too. They

keep your lungs from drying out.

Mucus glands are also found in the

pancreas (PAN-kree-us), an organ that

lies near the stomach. Its mucus helps break

down food so that your body can use it.

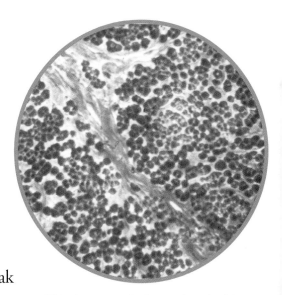

This tissue sample shows what the fibers that grow in the pancreas look like.

People with cystic fibrosis have cysts (SISTS) and fibers in their

pancreas instead of normal cells. A cyst is a tiny bunch of cells. A

fiber is a group of cells that form a string or cord.

The cysts and fibers are only part of the disease though. People

with CF have many health problems. Their mucus glands do not

work right. The mucus they make is too thick and sticky. This thick

mucus clogs up their lungs so people with CF have a hard time

breathing. They can never seem to get enough air. They cough a lot.

Too much mucus in the lungs makes breathing difficult and causes coughing.

Thick mucus also messes up a person's intestines. Normal intestines get **vitamins** and **nutrients** out of food as it goes through the body. In people with CF, however, the thick mucus keeps this from happening. As food goes through, only some of the nutrients are saved.

Almost everyone with CF has a problem with the glands that make sweat. The sweat they produce is much too salty. Some people with CF also get **growths** inside their noses. Others have heart problems.

Babies are born with this disease. Doctors might not notice it right away. Children may grow up and learn they have it years later. CF can be very mild or very severe. People with CF have it all their lives. Fifty years ago, a baby born with CF probably would not live to be two years old. Now, most people with the disease live to be at least 30. There is no cure, but people can learn how to live with CF.

People with CF learn how to eat properly so that they can get as many of the nutrients in food as possible into their bodies.

CHAPTER THREE

WHAT CAUSES CYSTIC FIBROSIS?

Through our genes, we inherit from our parents how we look and sometimes the diseases we get.

Children are born with cystic fibrosis because they have genes for

this disease. Genes are molecules in the body that make people what

they are. Everyone inherits their genes from their parents.

Some genes give people black hair. Some make people grow tall.

Some genes give people wide feet. And some genes give people cystic

fibrosis. When people have these genes, their mucus glands don't

work right.

CHAPTER FOUR

What's It Like to Have Cystic Fibrosis?

Living with cystic fibrosis can be tough. People with severe cystic fibrosis have a hard time getting enough air to breathe properly. They get tired quickly. They do not **digest** their food easily. People with mild cystic fibrosis, however, may not even know they have the disease. People have reached the age of 60 or 70 years without even knowing they had it!

The worst problem with cystic fibrosis is damage to the lungs. Little tubes inside the lungs get clogged with mucus so that not enough air can get in. Children with CF become breathless easily. They often have to stop and catch their breath. They cannot run around on the playground for long. Some people with CF have big chests. Their chest muscles work hard at breathing all the time.

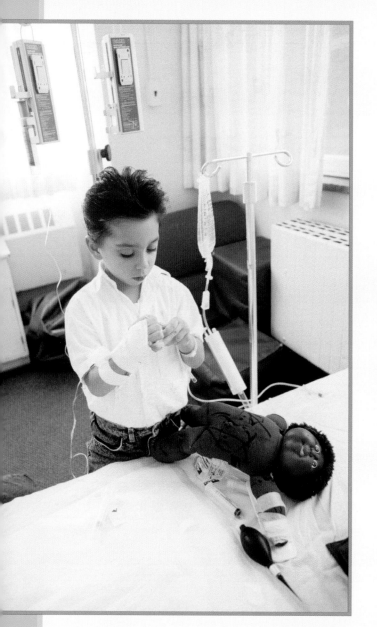

Kids with CF may have to go to the hospital several times a year because of lung infections.

People with cystic fibrosis often get lung **infections,** too. Mucus builds up in their lungs and they cannot get rid of it all by coughing. Germs enter their lungs and live in the mucus. These germs make people sick. People with CF have to take lots of medicine to kill the germs.

Children with CF may have to stay in the hospital several times a year. They go there to rest and get medicine for their lung infections.

People with CF have to eat larger meals and more snacks so that their bodies get enough vitamins and nutrients.

Children with CF also have some **digestion** problems.

They may eat as much as most children. But all their food does not

get broken down in their stomach and intestines. When food is not

broken down, the body cannot get all the vitamins and nutrients

from it.

Enzymes (EN-zymz) help to break down food. The pancreas

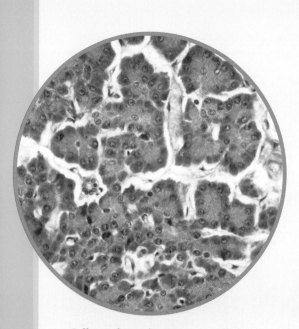

Cells made in the pancreas called enzymes help break down food in the stomach.

makes enzymes and pours them onto food after it leaves the stomach. In children with cystic fibrosis, however, sticky mucus gets in the way. Enzymes cannot reach the food, so the food is not broken down enough. Later in life, the pancreas may become full of cysts and fibers. Then it hardly produces any enzymes at all. Some children and adults with CF are very thin because their bodies are just not getting enough nutrients from their food. Other CF children might not grow as tall as their friends.

People with CF often eat extra-large meals. Sometimes they munch on snacks all day long. This way, they make up for all the food that does not get broken down. Sometimes they swallow enzyme pills with their meals. The enzymes go through their body with their food and start breaking it down.

At times, people with cystic fibrosis have to eat salty foods. By doing this, they replace all the salt they lose in their sweat.

Salty foods, such as potato chips, help kids with CF replace the salt that they lose through sweating.

Children with cystic fibrosis really like to have some special friends. When they go to the hospital, their friends come and do homework with them. When they spend the night, their friends make sure there are extra snacks around.

THE GIRL WHO
LIKED TO RACE

Kimberly Myers was a little girl who loved race cars. She liked their power and speed. She wanted to see what it was like to be in the driver's seat. She couldn't wait to zoom around a track. Kimberly wanted to race like "one of the boys."

When Kim was seventeen, the doctors told her she had cystic fibrosis. All of a sudden, her life changed. Now she might never get to race. She might have to give up her dreams. Kimberly spent a lot of time in the hospital taking medicines. She asked her doctors and nurses lots of questions. She learned all she could about the disease. She met other people with cystic fibrosis. Some were so sad about their disease that they just gave up their dreams. Kimberly decided that she would be different. She would race—no matter what.

Kimberly's boyfriend bought an old race car for her. Soon she was speeding around nearby tracks. Kim got better and better at racing. She loved the excitement. She loved to beat other racers.

She started telling other people with CF that they could follow
their dreams.

Kimberly won all kinds of racing awards. In 1997, she went
to the hospital for the last time. After she died, many children
said that Kimberly was their hero.

CHAPTER FIVE

WHAT CAN WE DO
ABOUT CYSTIC FIBROSIS?

People with CF often have salty tasting skin.

Many years ago, no one knew anything about cystic fibrosis. People

knew only that some babies tasted salty when they were kissed and

that those babies did not live long. In the 1700s, people thought a

salty child was bewitched. Books in the 1800s warned that salty-tasting children were **hexed.** They predicted that such children

would soon die.

In the 1900s, however, doctors started to figure things out. They

noticed that some children coughed a lot. They saw children who ate

plenty, but did not gain much

weight. And they saw that

many salty-tasting children

had these same problems.

In 1938, Dorothy

Andersen wrote a paper about

patients who had problems

with their pancreas. She

named the disease "cystic

fibrosis of the pancreas."

Dr. Dorothy Andersen was the doctor who named cystic fibrosis in 1938.

Slowly, doctors started putting everything together. In time, they realized that salty sweat, coughing, digestion problems, and a problem with the pancreas were all part of the same disease.

Now there is a sweat test that tells whether a person has cystic fibrosis. Doctors use a soft pad to get the sweat from a patient's arm. If there is too much salt, the person probably has CF.

Newborn babies do not usually get a sweat test, so their parents do not know if they have cystic fibrosis. Later, if a child coughs or is often breathless, the doctor will think of CF. The child is then given the sweat test to find out if CF is the cause.

Years ago, children with cystic fibrosis died before they were even old enough to go to school. No one knew how to help them. Today, we know many ways to treat children and adults. Now most people with CF live into their twenties, thirties, and forties.

People with

cystic fibrosis take

medicines or have

operations. They go

to **therapists**

(THER-uh-pists)

and learn how to deal

with their disease.

Some medicines can

be **inhaled** when

breathing is a

Some medicines that help people with CF are inhaled.

problem. These medicines may help widen the tubes in the lungs.

Other drugs help to thin out the mucus. Some drugs kill germs

living in the mucus.

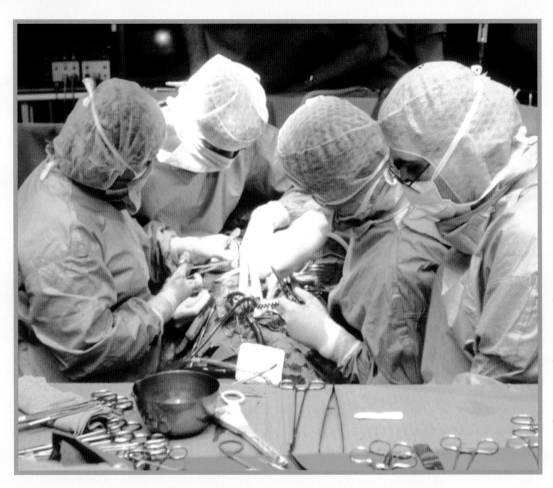

People with severe CF sometimes need to have a lung transplant.

People with severe lung problems might need a lung transplant.

They go to the hospital for this operation and get a whole new set of

lungs. The new lungs have normal mucus glands.

Usually, the digestive problems are not as serious as the lung

problems. They are also easier to treat. CF patients eat extra meat,

Eating extra meat and taking vitamins helps with the digestive problems caused by CF.

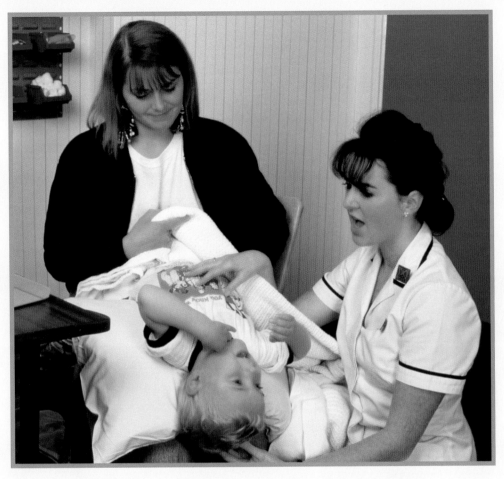

A therapist loosens the mucus in this boy's lungs through chest therapy.

fish, eggs, and cheese. They take extra vitamins. They take enzyme

pills with their meals.

Therapy and exercise are also important. Chest therapy helps to

loosen the mucus in the lungs. In chest therapy, a patient might lie

on a slanted bed with his or her head down. Someone else claps the

person on the chest or

back. There are also

machines that do this job.

They jiggle or pat the

patient while he or she

lies still. Soon the mucus

loosens up and the patient

gets rid of it by coughing.

Exercise helps, too.

Children might jump on

a trampoline to loosen

the mucus. Other exercises

can help kids with CF

stay in shape.

Exercise is a big help in keeping lungs free of mucus.

Scientists have created a nasal spray that helps the mucus glands in people with CF work better.

CHAPTER SIX

WILL WE EVER CURE CYSTIC FIBROSIS?

We are learning more about cystic fibrosis all the time. In 1989, scientists discovered the gene that causes cystic fibrosis. Now they have created a nose spray that contains the normal gene. When a CF patient uses the spray, the mucus glands in the nose work better.

Now scientists are working on a way to get the normal gene into a patient's lungs. They hope this will cure the mucus glands there. Other scientists are figuring out ways to keep the lung problems from happening at all. They are also working on the best ways to treat other body organs.

We have all come a long way since the 1700s. Today, no one thinks babies are hexed! Instead, we know about genes and enzymes. Perhaps, one day, cystic fibrosis will never be a problem for anyone.

Glossary

ancestors (AN-sess-turs) Your ancestors are your relatives who lived long ago, such as your grandfathers and great-grandfathers.

cells (SELS) Cells are the tiny building blocks that make up every organ in the body.

digest (dye-JEST) To digest means to break down food so that the body can use it.

digestion (duh-JESS-chuhn) Digestion is the process by which the body breaks down food after it is eaten.

growths (GROHTHS) Growths are lumps of tissue.

hexed (HEKSD) Someone hexed is thought to be under an evil spell or bewitched.

infections (in-FEK-shuhns) Infections are illnesses caused by germs that invade the body.

intestines (in-TESS-tins) Intestines are the long tubes in the body that digest food.

inhaled (in-HAYLD) Something inhaled is breathed in.

nutrients (NOO-tree-uhnts) Nutrients are the materials the body needs to grow and work right.

therapists (THER-uh-pists) Therapists are people who treat an illness or injury.

vitamins (VYE-thu-mins) Vitamins are important chemicals the body needs to be healthy.

Questions and Answers about Cystic Fibrosis

If someone with cystic fibrosis coughs a lot, can I catch their disease? No, that cannot happen. They have cystic fibrosis because they got the CF genes from their parents. This is the only way anyone gets CF.

My friend at school has CF. Will he ever get well? Your friend will always have the disease. He can do things to help himself live with it, however. He will probably get used to doing special exercises. He will take extra helpings at meals and might need medicine from time to time.

What's the hardest part of having CF? For someone with CF, it is scary when they cannot get enough air. They might breathe very hard and fast, but that just doesn't seem to be enough.

Helping a Friend Who Has Cystic Fibrosis

Watch and see what your friend has trouble with. Maybe running games make him breathless at recess. You could think up other games to play. You might also visit him when he has to go to the hospital. You could do homework with him so that he does not get behind.

Did You Know?

▸ Every year, about 2,500 babies are born with cystic fibrosis.

▸ Most people with CF have **ancestors** who lived in northern Europe.

▸ Often, children with CF cannot pronounce its name. Instead of cystic fibrosis, they say they have "65 roses." Kimberly Myers gave her race car the number 65. She painted the word "roses" next to the 65. This was her way of telling people about the disease.

How to Learn More about Cystic Fibrosis

At the Library: Nonfiction
Gold, Susan Dudley.
Cystic Fibrosis.
New York: Crestwood House, 2000.

Henry, Cynthia S., and Tom Dineen (Illustrator).
Taking Cystic Fibrosis to School.
Valley Park, Mo.: JayJo Books, 2000.

Lee, Justin.
Everything You Need to Know about Cystic Fibrosis.
New York: Rosen Publishing Group, 2001.

Silverstein, Alvin.
Cystic Fibrosis.
New York: Franklin Watts, 1994.

Woodson, Meg.
Turn It into Glory: A Mother's Moving Story of Her Daughter's Last Great Adventure.
Minneapolis, Minn.: Bethany House Publishers, 1991.

At the Library: Fiction
Arnold, Katrin.
Anna Joins In.
Nashville, Tenn.: Abingdon Press, 1982.

Grishaw, Joshua, and Lane Yerkes (Illustrator).
My Heart is Full of Wishes.
Austin, Tex.: Raintree/Steck-Vaughn, 2000.

Radley, Gail.
CF in His Corner.
New York: Four Winds Press, 1984.

On the Web

Visit our home page for lots of links about cystic fibrosis:
http://www.childsworld.com/links.html

Note to Parents, Teachers, and Librarians: We routinely verify our Web links to make sure they're safe, active sites—so encourage your readers to check them out!

Through the Mail or by Phone

Center for Gene Therapy of Cystic Fibrosis and Other Genetic Diseases
University of Iowa Health Care
3 Lions Drive
North Liberty, IA 52317
319/665-2111

The Cystic Fibrosis Foundation
6931 Arlington Road, #200
Bethesda, MD 20814
301/951-4422 or 800/344-4823
http://www.cff.org

Cystic Fibrosis Research Inc.
Bayside Business Plaza
2672 Bayshore Parkway
Suite 520
Mountain View, CA 94043
650/404-9975

March of Dimes Birth Defects Foundation
1275 Mamaroneck Avenue
White Plains, NY 10605
888/663-4637

National Heart, Lung, and Blood Institute (NHLBI)
NHLBI Health Information Network
P.O. Box 30105
Bethesda, MD 20824-0105
301/592-8573 or 800/327-5605

Index

About the Author

Susan H. Gray has a bachelor's degree and a master's degree in zoology. She has taught college-level biology, anatomy, and physiology classes. In her 25 years as an author, she has written medical articles, science papers, and children's books. Ms. Gray especially enjoys writing on scientific topics for children, as it is a challenge to present complex material to young readers. In addition to her children's books, she writes grant proposals for several organizations. Ms. Gray lives with her husband, Michael, in Cabot, Arkansas. She enjoys playing the piano, traveling, and gardening.